Making Fractions

© Aladdin Books Ltd 1998
Produced by
Aladdin Books Ltd
28 Percy Street
London W1P OLD

First published in
the United States
in 1998 by
Copper Beech Books,
an imprint of
The Millbrook Press
2 Old New Milford Road
Brookfield, Connecticut 06804

Project Editor: Sally Hewitt
Editor: Liz White
Design: David West Children's Book Design
Designer: Simon Morse
Photography: Roger Vlitos
Illustrator: Tony Kenyon

**Library of Congress
Cataloging-in-Publication Data**

King, Andrew, 1961-
Making fractions / by Andrew King ; illustrated by Tony Kenyon.
p. cm. — (Math for fun)
Includes index.
Summary: Explores the different ways fractions of a whole can be
expressed—as fractions, decimals, percentages, and ratios.
ISBN 0-7613-0723-0 (lib. bdg.).
— ISBN 0-7613-0732-X (pbk.)
1. Fractions—Juvenile literature.
[1. Fractions.] I. Kenyon, Tony, ill. II. Title.
III. Series: King, Andrew, 1961- Math for fun.
QA117.K56 1998   97-41603
513.2'6—dc21   CIP AC

MATH *for fun*

Making Fractions

Andrew King

Copper Beech Books
Brookfield, Connecticut

CONTENTS

INTRODUCTION

It's amazing what you can do if you know your fractions.
You can use percentages, proportions, and ratios with ease.
If you are told that nine-tenths of an iceberg is
hidden underwater, can you imagine what that looks
like? If your sweater is made
of 100% pure wool, do you
know what that means?

Try out the exciting activities, practical
projects, and games in this book and you
can have fun learning about fractions.

● Follow the STEP-BY-STEP INSTRUCTIONS to help you
carry out the activities.

● Use the HELPFUL HINTS for clues to help you with
the experiments and games.

● Look at MORE IDEAS for information about other
projects for you to try.

1 Yellow squares mean this is
an easy activity.

2 Blue squares mean this is a
medium activity.

3 Red squares mean this is
a hard activity.

WHAT IS A FRACTION?

A **fraction** is a part of a **whole** thing like a cake, an apple, or a school class. If a cake has had a slice cut out of it, it is not whole. The slice is a part, or a fraction, of the whole cake. If an apple is cut up, it

is not a whole. The pieces are fractions of the whole.

APPLE GETS THE CHOP

1 This apple has been cut into two equal pieces. It has been cut in **half**. A half is a fraction and we write it like this $\frac{1}{2}$.

2 This apple has been cut into four equal pieces. It has been cut into quarters. A quarter is a fraction too. We write it like this $\frac{1}{4}$.

PIZZA SLICES

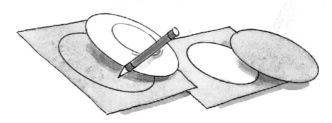

1 Trace around a plate on construction paper to make two circles. Decorate both circles like a pizza and cut them out.

2 Fold one pizza exactly in half. Cut along the fold to make two halves.

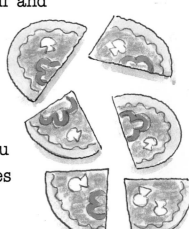

3 Repeat step 2 for the second pizza. Now fold each half exactly in half and cut along the folds to make four quarters.

4 How many ways can you fit your pizza slices together to make a whole?

MORE IDEAS

● Try to put three quarters and one half together. You will get one pizza with a quarter left over. You can write this as $1\frac{1}{4}$ or as a fraction $\frac{5}{4}$. Fractions bigger than a whole are called **improper fractions.**

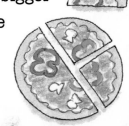

ADDING FRACTIONS

Fractions can be added like any other number. To make a whole pizza (see page 7,) you needed to add the fractions of the pizza together. There are many different ways of adding fractions together to make a whole.

BUILD A FRACTION WALL

1 These children are building a fraction wall using blocks of different sizes. You can make a small fraction wall from colored cardboard.

2 Copy these shapes onto the cardboard and cut them all out. You need one whole block, two 1/2 blocks, three 1/3 blocks, four 1/4 blocks, five 1/5 blocks, and six 1/6 blocks.

1/6

1/5

1/4

1/3

1/2

1

1/3 1/6

1/2 1/6

1/4 1

Remember that each layer of the wall must be exactly equal to a whole block.

3 You can use these blocks to build your own wall. Start with the whole block on the bottom and build your wall using a mixture of fractions.

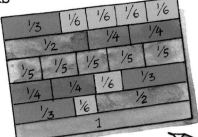

HELPFUL HINTS
● Match all the layers against the whole block. If they fit exactly the sum is correct.

MORE IDEAS
● When the wall is as high as possible, write down the fraction names of the blocks you have used on each layer.
● Extend your wall by making other fraction blocks. How about a ninth — $1/9$?

9

FAIR SHARES

A fraction can also be part of a group of things. Have you ever been asked to share some candy with your brother or sister? When you have divided the candy equally with another person you have divided the candy in half. A half is a fraction of the whole group of candy.

GRAB!

This is a fun fraction game for two, three, or four players. You will need about 50 small pieces or you could use dried beans.

1 Put the pieces in a container. The first player grabs a handful of beans.

2 Try to divide the handful into two equal groups or halves. If you can, you score two points.

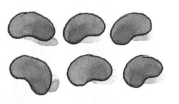

= 2 points.

3 Can you divide the beans into four equal groups, or quarters? If you can, score four more points.

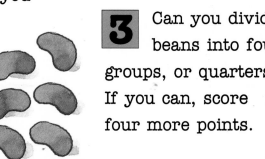

= 4 points.

4 If you can complete steps 1, 2, and 3 you can go on to the bonus round! If you can divide your beans into three equal groups, or thirds, score a bonus of three points.

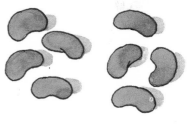

= **3 points.**

5 When you have taken a turn, put the beans back and the next player takes a turn.

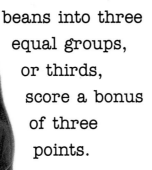

MORE IDEAS

● Is 17 a good number to grab? What about 16? What about 12? Which would earn you the higher score?

● Keep playing the game. Note down the numbers that score the most points. Can you discover the numbers that are best for sharing into equal groups

DECIMAL FRACTIONS

Decimals are another way of writing fractions. You have probably seen a lot of decimal numbers before without realizing! If you have watched any sporting events on television, the distances jumped or thrown are usually shown as a decimal number.

9.83

A decimal number is one with a **decimal point.** The point separates the whole numbers on the left from the numbers less than 1 on the right.

1 There are ten tenths between 0 and 1. The object of this game is to point to the correct place on the number line.

POINT IT OUT
Try this guessing game with your friends.

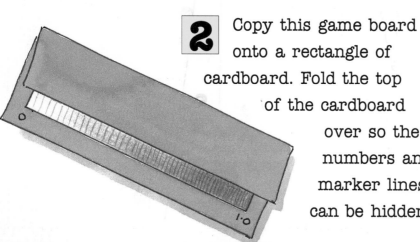

0   0·1   0·2   0·3   0·4   0·5   0·6   0·7   0·8   0·9   1·0

2 Copy this game board onto a rectangle of cardboard. Fold the top of the cardboard over so the numbers and marker lines can be hidden.

1·0

3 The first player covers the side showing the tenths and asks the second player to find a decimal from 0.1 to 0.9. It could be 0.4 for example. The second player has to estimate where it might be on the number line.

4 Uncover the line and see if they managed to point it out!

MORE IDEAS

● If you have a calculator, find out what happens if you try to show a half on the display.

The buttons you need to press to do this are 1÷2=. You will see 0.5 on the display. Do the same with a quarter, 1÷4=. You will see 0.25.

Try other fractions and see what happens.

● What happens if you try 1÷5? What fraction is this?

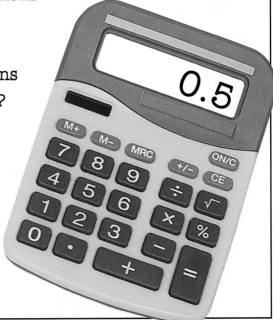

LARGER OR SMALLER?

How do you decide if one decimal number is larger than another? With whole numbers like 134 and 273 you can compare the size of the digits starting on the left. 273 is bigger than 134 because the 2 digit is worth more than the 1 digit. You can compare decimal numbers like 23.75 and 14.28 in the same way.

DIABOLICAL DECIMALS

1 The object of this game is to make the largest number. If you win draw a happy face. First draw a chart like this one. The first player throws the die and decides where to place the digit.

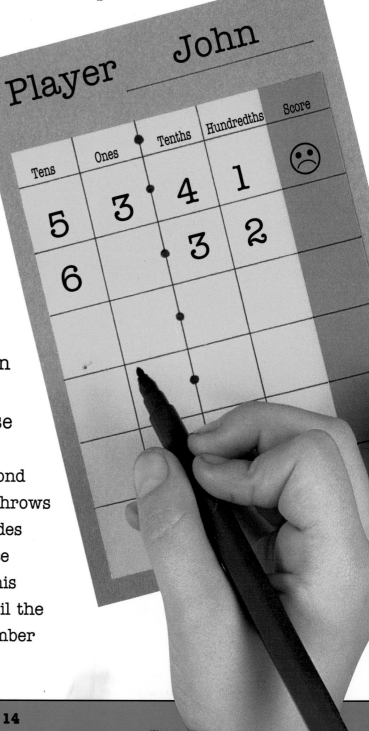

Player				John	
Tens	Ones	Tenths	Hundredths	Score
5	3	4	1	☹
6		3	2	

= You win

= You lose

2 Remember to put a big digit on the left. Where would you put a 5? Be careful, you might throw a 6 next turn!

3 The second player throws and also decides where to place their digit. This continues until the four digit number is completed.

It's Emma's turn to throw. Who do you think will win this game?

HELPFUL HINTS

● To find out who has won compare the digits on the left. If they are the same move to the next digits to their right. If they still match repeat the process until you have found out who has made the larger number.

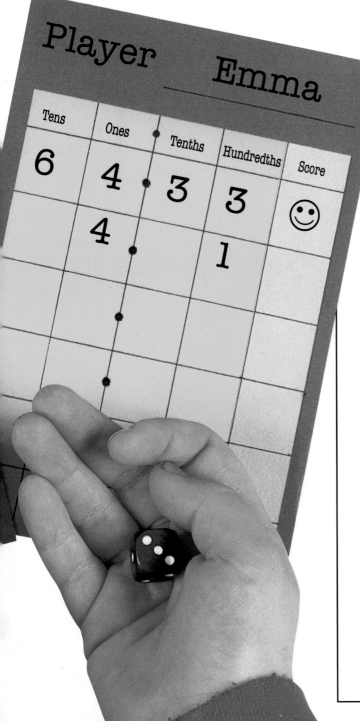

Player _____ Emma

Tens	Ones	Tenths	Hundredths	Score
6	4	3	3	☺
	4		1	

MORE IDEAS

● There are some interesting variations to Diabolical decimals that you can play.

● The winner could be the player who makes the smallest number.

● You can also play a game in teams of two. Take turns to throw the die and try to get your numbers as close together as possible. The winning team is the one with the smallest difference between their pairs of numbers. Use a calculator to check.

Team 1
4	3	6	2	☺
4	2	5	1	

Team 2
6	2	6	5	☹
6	5	6	3	

ADDING DECIMALS

Adding decimal numbers is as easy as adding whole numbers. The key to making it easy is remembering to add digits from the same position in the number system. In other words, adding tens to tens, ones to ones, tenths to tenths and hundredths to hundredths.

> **If the answer to 23 + 34 = 57 then 2.3 + 3.4 = 5.7**

SPLOTCH IT!
This game is all about adding up tenths. Tenths are shown by the first digit to the right of the decimal point. Remember, ten tenths make 1.

1 Make a set of splotch cards. Cut out a stack of 20 splodges from some colored cardboard.

2 Write in the numbers. Make sure the numbers on the edges of the splotch all add up to the total in the center.

3 Take turns to hold up a splotch card with one of the corners covered.

HELPFUL HINTS
● To make sure you are putting the correct totals in the center of your cards it might be a good idea to use a calculator to check the answer. Remember to press the decimal point!

4 Can your opponent work out what the hidden number is? You could solve it like this $0.2+0.3+?=1$.

MORE IDEAS
● You could change this game around by covering the total in the middle. Are you still as good?
● See if you can figure out what is in the middle of this card. You could try to solve it like this $0.6+0.3+1.1=?$.

1.1

0.6

0.3

PERCENTAGES

Percentages are a way of showing fractions as a part of one hundred. A half of a hundred is fifty. We call fifty out of a hundred, fifty percent. The symbol mathematicians use for percent looks like this %. Twenty-five is a quarter of a hundred, so a quarter can be written as 25%. A **tenth** of a hundred is 10. How do you think a tenth would be written as a percentage?

PERCENTAGE PATTERNS

Take a look at this hundred square. Each one of the small squares represents 1%.

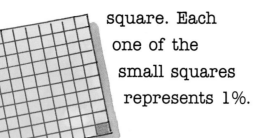

1 If half of the hundred square is filled in, 50 squares will be covered, or 50%.

2 We could show 50% like this, but there are many fun ways to show it on a hundred square!

3 Find some graph paper and see if you can design an unusual pattern that covers exactly 50% of the hundred square.

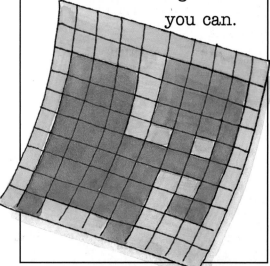

HELPFUL HINTS

● For 50% of the hundred square to be covered you must color 50 small squares. When you plan your design mark the squares lightly with a pencil. It is easier to make a change if you have miscounted!

MORE IDEAS

● Try some different percentage amounts to cover your hundred square. What about a design that shows 30% of the square? How about 51%?

● Make your design as interesting as you can.

ESTIMATING PERCENTAGES

Making an **estimate** is like making a careful guess. People make estimates using percentages.

If a teacher says "about fifty percent of the class have done their homework" she estimates that about half the class have done it!

$$\frac{Amount}{Whole} \times 100 = Percentage$$

HOW SQUARE ARE YOUR EYES?
This hundred square represents the whole day, 24 hours. You can make your own one to find out how you spend your time.

1 You will need a plain piece of square paper and some coloring pens to fill in your own grid.

First, fold the paper in half and keep folding in strips. Unfold the paper and fold in the other direction. Open out the paper and you will find that you have made squares. Mark out a big square of 10x10 small squares to make a hundred square grid.

At School

Sleeping

Eating

2 Estimate the percentage of time you think you spend watching T.V. Shade in your estimate on the grid. For example, if you think it is 5%, color in five squares on the grid.

3 Next, estimate the percentage of the day spent doing other things like eating, sleeping, playing, and working. Shade in the amounts on your hundred square.

Make a list of your estimates like this before you color your grid.

Sleeping	7%
Eating	45%
Playing	15%
School	23%
T.V.	10%

T.V. guide

Watching T.V.

Playing

HELPFUL HINTS
● Make sure your whole hundred square gets covered. There shouldn't be any gaps — you are always doing something, even if it is sleeping!
● Use a different bright color for each activity.

4 Compare your finished hundred square with the one in this picture. Have you estimated that you are sleepier or more wide awake?!

MORE IDEAS
● How good is your estimate?
● Find an older friend or an adult who is really good at math. Ask them to calculate the real percentages of how you spend your day!
● How does your estimate compare?

MAKING 100%

Have you ever heard of anything being described as 100% pure or 100% genuine? 100% means everything, the whole. The whole doesn't have to be made up of 100 separate pieces. Do you remember that 50% is another way of describing a half? 50% of 80 is 40. 50% of 36 is 18. What is 50% of 90?

MAGIC CARPETS
Some traditional carpet designs from around the world use many colors and patterns.

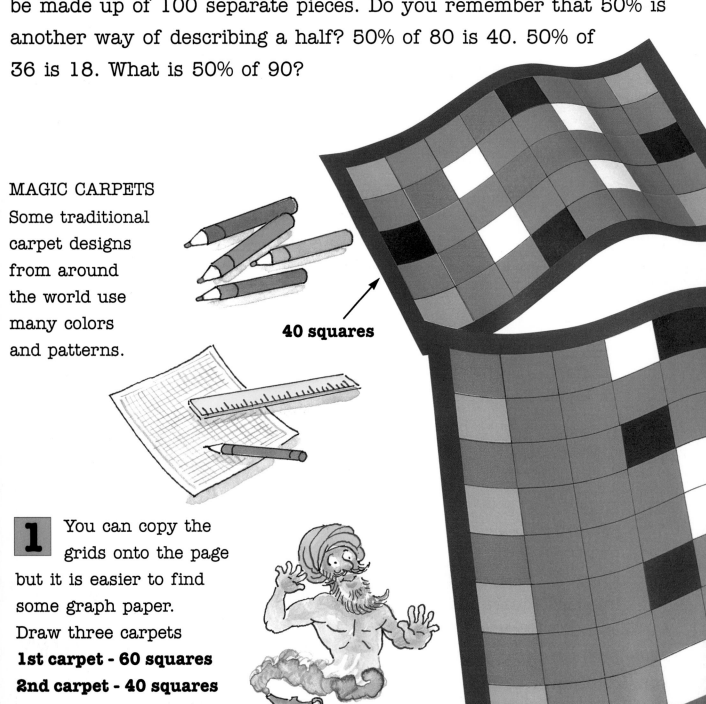

40 squares

1 You can copy the grids onto the page but it is easier to find some graph paper. Draw three carpets

1st carpet - 60 squares
2nd carpet - 40 squares
3rd carpet - 80 squares

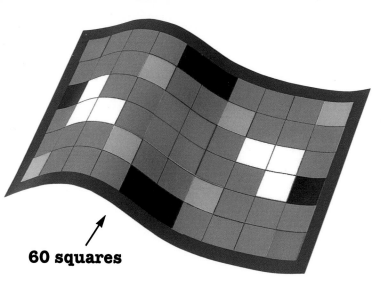

60 squares

2 Design your own carpet pattern using six colors. Your design must be 50% blue, 10% red, 10% yellow, 10% green, 10% black, 10% white. Check the percentages that have been used for the carpets in this picture.

HELPFUL HINTS

● If you are stuck, find out what 50% of your carpet is.

● For the first carpet of 60 squares, 50% is half the total — which is 30 squares!

● To find 10% divide the total, 60 by 10. This gives the answer 6. So, 30 squares will be blue, 6 red, 6 yellow, 6 green, 6 black, and 6 white.

80 squares

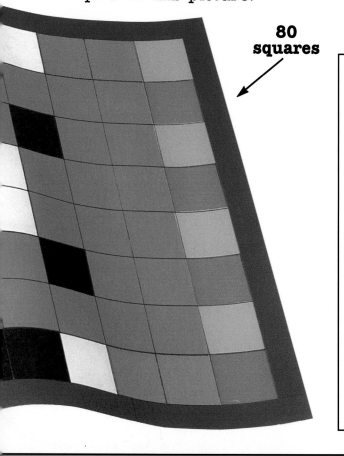

MORE IDEAS

● Design some more carpets. This time make them more intricate by dividing some squares in half.

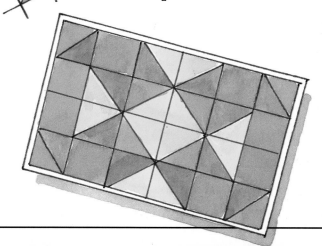

RATIOS

Ratios can be used to show the amounts in which different things are combined to make a whole. Paints are very often made up of mixtures of the primary colors — red, blue, and yellow. To get an exact shade they are mixed according to a particular ratio. Two parts red to one part blue makes purple. The parts can be measured with teaspoons. You would write it like this 2:1 red blue.

MIXING IT

1 You can make your own color chart by some careful mixing. Choose two colors.

2 Make a chart showing where you will paint your different tints. Show the ratio of different paints you will use.

Red : Yellow

Red

3:2

1:1

2:7

1:8

Yellow

3 If you are mixing paints in the ratio of 3:2 use a small spoon to measure out three parts red to two parts yellow and mix carefully.

4 Paint a small sample of the different mixtures into each area to complete your reference chart.

HELPFUL HINTS

● When you are mixing the colors make sure the amount you use for each part is always the same! The easiest way to make sure you are accurate is to use a teaspoon that you can level off with a piece of cardboard.

● When you have used one mixture make sure you wash your brush carefully, otherwise you will finish up with muddy looking colors that all look the same!

MORE IDEAS

● Find different ways of mixing the three primary colors together.

● What does 1 red : 4 yellow : 1 blue look like?

● Which is your favorite color? What is the ratio of the three colors?

● Try to work out the ratios of the color of your favorite crayon. Use different ratios until you can find a match.

MORE MIXING

Ratios can also show how more than two quantities can be mixed. You probably use ratios a lot without realizing it. If you wanted to record how flour, butter, and sugar were combined to make some cookies it could be written like this 3:2:2 three parts flour, two parts butter, and two parts sugar. The parts could be measured with cups or spoons. You could do the same for mixing drinks.

SHAKEN NOT STIRRED
You can make some fantastic fruit drinks by mixing ingredients carefully!

1 Try starting with orange juice, apple juice, and seltzer. A delicious combination is five parts apple, two parts orange, and three parts seltzer. You can make the drink like this.

2 First find a small container, like an eggcup, and a large glass. Fill the eggcup, or the measurer you have chosen, five times with apple juice and tip it into the glass.

3 Now add two eggcups of the orange juice.

Apple	Orange	Seltzer	Good/Bad?
5	2	3	Excellent

4 Last of all pour in three eggcups of seltzer. Stir it and taste. Mmmmm....

5 What do you think? Now try your own mixture.

HELPFUL HINTS

● Remember to keep a careful note of the number of parts you have mixed together and the mixtures you liked. You might want to note this in a table.

MORE IDEAS

● What about trying other ingredients to make that perfect drink? You could try some other fruit juices, lemonade can be nice, or what about a little vinegar!

● Make sure you ask an adult if you want to try these or any other ingredients in your drink.

PERFECTLY PROPORTIONED

Many things in nature, including people, grow in a very precise way. For example, the size of everyone's head has a particular relationship, or proportion, to their height. If you measure around your head and multiply that length by three, the answer you get will be roughly the same as your height.

ARE YOU SIX FEET TALL?
You may not believe it but you are about six feet tall! In fact, nearly everyone is! Using ratios you can prove that most people are about six feet tall.

1 Find a long strip of cardboard or paper and ask an adult to stand next to it. Have the adult take off a shoe. Place the heel of the shoe on the floor, toe pointing upward against the cardboard.

2 Mark where the end of the toe is with a pen then move the shoe up so that the heel is where your finger is.

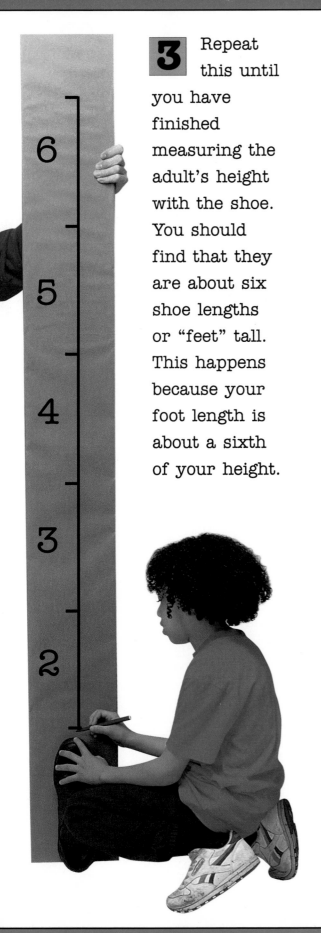

3 Repeat this until you have finished measuring the adult's height with the shoe. You should find that they are about six shoe lengths or "feet" tall. This happens because your foot length is about a sixth of your height.

HELPFUL HINTS

● The proportions of younger growing bodies are not usually the same as an adult's. You can try this with your friends but it might be more reliable to test it on an adult.

MORE IDEAS

● Another fascinating body ratio is sometimes known as Pythagoras's navel. This ratio compares a person's height with the height of the navel from the ground.

● It is usually in the ratio of 1:1.6

● This is a very special ratio called the Golden Mean. It is often found in nature and was considered by the ancient Greeks to have divine properties.

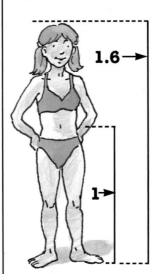

1.6 →

1 →

● Measure your height, then the height of your navel from the floor. Divide the first height by the second. How close to 1.6 is the result? Is your body of divine proportion?

FRACTION WALL

| ⅑ | ⅑ | ⅑ | ⅑ | ⅑ | ⅑ | ⅑ | ⅑ | ⅑ |

| ⅛ | ⅛ | ⅛ | ⅛ | ⅛ | ⅛ | ⅛ | ⅛ |

| ⅐ | ⅐ | ⅐ | ⅐ | ⅐ | ⅐ | ⅐ |

| ⅙ | ⅙ | ⅙ | ⅙ | ⅙ | ⅙ |

| ⅕ | ⅕ | ⅕ | ⅕ | ⅕ |

| ¼ | ¼ | ¼ | ¼ |

| ⅓ | ⅓ | ⅓ |

| ½ | ½ |

| 1 |

GLOSSARY

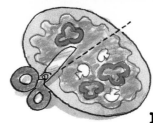

Decimal
We use a decimal number system. That means that we count in ones and groups of tens.

Decimal point
A decimal point separates the digits worth 1 or more on the left from digits less than 1 on the right. A decimal number looks like this 426.25.

Estimate
An estimate is a careful guess. You could estimate how many petals you think there are on a daisy. When you have made an estimate, you could check it by counting the petals.

Fraction
A fraction is part of a whole thing. A slice of pizza is a fraction of the whole pizza. A fraction looks like this: $3/4$. The top number tells us how many parts of the whole there are in the fraction. The bottom number tells us how many parts the whole has been divided into.

Half
A half is a fraction. We write it like this: $1/2$. You get two halves when you divide something into two equal parts.

Improper fraction
Fractions bigger than a whole are called improper fractions. $5/4$ is an improper fraction because the number on the top is larger than the number on the bottom.

Percentage
A percentage is a part of a hundred. A percent sign looks like this: %. 1% means 1 out of a hundred. 25% means 25 out of a hundred.

Ratio
A ratio is a way of comparing the amount of different things in a whole. If you mix two teaspoons of yellow paint to one teaspoon of red paint to make orange, you have used the ratio of 2:1 in your mixture.

Tenth
If you divide something into ten equal parts, one of those parts is a tenth. A tenth can look like this: $1/10$. The number after a decimal point shows you tenths. So the digit 6, in this decimal number 1.6, is 6 tenths.

Whole
Something that is whole has not been divided into parts or had anything taken away from it. A whole can be one thing like a pizza or it can be a group like a class of thirty children.

INDEX